Elise Stuart
www.elisestuart.com

Another Door Calls

Another Door Calls

Elise Stuart

Another Door Calls
Copyright ©2017 Elise Stuart

ISBN: 978-1-940769-66-0
Publisher: Mercury HeartLink
Silver City, New Mexico
Printed in the United States of America

Back cover photograph of author, Michael Cook.
Interior photographs for section headings, Glenn Henderson.

All rights reserved. This book, or sections of this book,
may not be reproduced or transmitted in any form
without permission from the author.

Permission is granted to educators to create copies of
individual poems for classroom or workshop assignments
with proper acknowledgment and credits.

Contact the author at *elisestuart16@gmail.com*

ANOTHER DOOR CALLS

Dedication	xi
Acknowledgements	xiii
Introduction	xv

CLUES ARE IN THE WILD PLACES

Entering the Wild	2
Look Out to Look In	4
The River Meets Itself	6
River	8
View	10
Strength of Clouds	12
Swept Away	14
The simple act of rain	16
Enchanted Mountain Peak	18

WHISPER ME TO STAY

At Night	22
Lightning	24
Reading the Stars	26
The Balance	28
Song of Gila	30
Attempted Relationship	32
Revisit	34
One	36
Opening	38

LIGHTNING SPLITS THE SKY

Another Door Calls to Me	42
Alive	46
The Place Between Light and Dark	48
Reality	50
Everything Begins in the Dark	52
Staying to the middle	54
Underground	56
Heartbeat of Sound	58

DREAMING HOME

New Voice	62
Lost	64
Three deer	66
Small Bird	68
My Dog Begins to Look Like a Wolf	70
All the little things	72
How it begins, how it ends	74
Dreaming Home	76
About the Author	81

to the
spirit of life
that nourishes
and connects
every living thing

and to the ones
who believed:
Gianna, Lisbeth, Stewart
JJ, Bonnie, Larry, Elvira

I would like to acknowledge
Glenn Henderson for his
magnificent photographs
and enduring support.

Introduction

My poetry is tied to the land. Stubborn land, this part of southwest New Mexico, where plants can survive with so little water. It makes me notice each weed and wildflower. It makes me look at myself more closely. In the direct gaze of the sun, the shadow side's seen more clearly. Not much allowance for secret-keeping, at least not from myself. The intensity of light bears down like a magnifying glass on what I've kept hidden. This land, with its wild beauty, some parts of it sharp and harsh, other parts tender and fragile, calls for diving deep into the nature of being.

ANOTHER

DOOR

CALLS

Clues Are in the Wild Places

Entering the Wild

Entering the wild you go back
to the time before this time...
It was always this way,
when you walked the paths slowly,
gathered by the river to wash,
looked into each others' eyes,
spoke without words.

Walking through the bright wide open,
you see a narrow path and turn to follow.
Down in the creek bed,
sudden shade greets you from both sides.
Sweeping your eyes along the banks,
looking for tracks in the sand,
listening for the sounds, the scurry of animals.
Above your head, trees are your canopy,
a bird calls out his song, over and over.

You keep walking through an old pear orchard,
a steep slope carries you down
and you hear
a waterfall, splashing quietly,
trickling down over rocks,
flowing into a shallow stream at the bottom.

Water cools your feet.
You listen. Only the sound of water...
You breathe. This place is like the place inside
that becomes real when you trust.

Entering the wild, you are not afraid.
You have never known fear.

The broken branch, hanging limp from above,
the soft, green leaves of the mullein,
growing in the shape of a curve,
the shattered egg shell
of some small bird.

You see the world in a new way.
Each leaf, each animal, each heart, your heart
is perfect, full of beauty, with all its imperfections.
This is a place where the truth of wild beauty still exists.
This is a place where everything teaches you.

Look Out to Look In

Love brings us up
from deep water to shore,
not a foot print for miles,
washes us up, gasping for air.

We look out, wanting to get love,
only to find our beloved is mirror, not source.
And all the while, love dwells beneath
the hard carapace of our hearts.

Clues are in the wild places . . .

The river meanders,
calmly agreeing with everything that happens.
Heavy rain slices its banks, changes its course,
yet it keeps on flowing.

The seed, hidden inside last year's flower head,
hangs on 'til just the right moment
when the wind whisks by
and drops it into rain-softened soil.

The endless search stops
when there is no need to look out.
We are not afraid to look in—to accept
our own broken, beautiful, beating heart.

The River Meets Itself

Long walk through woods,
soft and deep,
to get to this place.
Now see myself a part of the wild.

Green-brown water
coming this way,
flowing over rocks,
pale gray, russet-red.

White foam
becomes a bubbling spiral,
swirling
by a knob of land.

Two streams prepare
to meet in the midst of a river,
predestined forces
coming together.

We see each other,
recognize the light
that hides behind
any sadness in our eyes.
Point of convergence.

River

She loves all—
the birds, who dip in to catch their food, and sing to her,
the insects and lizards, who scurry on her banks,
the fish who swim within her,
and the humans,
with their conflicts and desires.

She is a mirror to many who walk beside her.
They see who they're afraid to be, who they wish to be,
sometimes, who they really are.
Truths they utter fall silently into the river,
making an arc of ripples throughout.
Lies fall, like heavy stones, to the bottom,
to bury themselves in mud,
the silky water always moving through anything
that tries to hold it.

She can take the wounded ones,
who hold their heads in their hands, looking down,
even the sad ones, who lie face-down.
She turns them gently, lifting their faces toward the sun
again.
Later—when they walk into her waters,
she holds them, awakens them with cold eddies,
kisses them with small warm pools.
Her grace extends towards them eternally.

Sometimes drought comes, dries her up,
yet she gives all she has.
The river will run—
moving underground if it must,
appearing parched and dry, but still alive.
She knows how to forgive any hurtful thing,
any act of violence.
The continuous flow, her answer.

View

High in the rocks,
in the wind,
surrounded by long
stretches of far desert,
we find a place
to sit above the trail.

Sun covers this haven—
stone desk,
grass rug, rock walls,
boundless blue ceiling,
a look-out.

Boulders, twenty feet tall,
stand on their heads,
feet in the air,
seemingly dropped here
by an unseen hand.

Stones, carved and pitted
by wind and rain
tell ancient stories
reaching back
millions of years

when all this land
was lake-river-sea.
Lay ear to stone,
the sound of water rushing
below.

Above, a hawk
rides waves of air,
black-tipped wings angled to earth,
showing us what it is
to be free.

As he rights himself,
we regain our fragile balance,
walk among the rocks,
feel our hearts leap—
from earth to sky.

Strength of Clouds

Heavy gray vapor quietly
covers the white,
all the way out to the edges,
wispy and blurred.
Diamond-shaped hole
reveals an underbelly of blue,
the true color of sky.
Watching the clouds surrender,
opening themselves until
absolutely full,
then sigh and let go.
They breathe in again, then out—
not afraid of the emptiness.

Embracing water with whiteness
'til arms become so heavy—
they sweep their palms downward,
like swans' wings before they ascend,
and allow tiny droplets of water
to pour down,
to plummet onto each waiting leaf,
each prickly stem and petal of the zinnia,
the smooth red skin of the plum,
then fall into the dry brown soil.

Swept Away

Muddy brown music,
the turbulent waters rush.
When you are in it,
let your head fall backward,
your hair, splayed out like seaweed,
becomes part of the river.

Let the current carry you as far as it can.
Find a rock to slow yourself,
feel it slide through your grasp.
Seek another handhold.
This time dig your fingers into
the mud at the bottom of the riverbed . . .
There's nothing to hold you.

Churning brown water sweeps
everything clean.
How tempting, how impossible,
to try to hang on to
what you must
let go of.

THE SIMPLE ACT OF RAIN

Rain has changed the landscape in a fortnight,
painted the hills green,
filled the river to the top of her banks
the water brown and roiling.

Dry barren land of the desert,
baked each day in persistent sun,
has changed so easily, so sweetly,
absorbing raindrops, until they are her own.

Through the simple act of rain,
the desert is forgiven her ways,
and becomes green again.

Across the river there are hoof beats,
a dapple-gray horse runs flat out
her feet pounding the earth. Shaking her mane,
she shies away from her own darkness.
How far can she run?

There is peace in the way the current moves,
swirling, still fast,
taking with it all that comes from the past
and slamming it into the present
so everything can move forward together,
sunlight shimmering on the surface,
to become something new.

Enchanted Mountain Peak

On the peak of the mountain,
my feet touch earth.
My arms reach upward
toward the pale yellow glow of sunset,
and the full moon, rising.

The sun, moon and I connect
in a singular triangle on this high peak,
then suddenly, pale gold's gone,
darkness falls.

Alone on the mountaintop
can't see the way down.
Stumble on rocky ground,
hear the sound of water,
a creek?

Follow, hoping it will lead me out.
Lights of small houses appear.
Knock on a door, we speak two
separatelanguages
yet we understand each other.

Estas perdido?
Nodding...
Vamos a ayudar le.
Gracias—heartfelt.
They drive me to a hippie's adobe house.

From the pure light
of communing with
moon, earth, sun,
down to the dark fear of
being alone and lost . . .

The land of New Mexico
reveals my inner life,
teaches me to trust her,
then brings me home
in her own way.

Whisper Me to Stay

At Night

Lying beneath a thick comforter
and far-off stars,
I move over a little,
making my body a separate island.

Illness drives a wedge
between me and the world.
I crave solitude,
its calm, drifting rhythm.

Only in the dark,
edges begin to blur.
Close my eyes and become
more than this body.

'Round a bend to stand in golden light.
Recall touching the pale down
on my son's tiny head,
right at the crown,

soft spot that dimples in
where Soul
dives into the body
and flies out.

Lightning

Finally, deep in the night
the wind picks up,
dark clouds break open
and rain begins.

Stepping under the skylight
a silver flash lights me,
illumines me—
after a long spell of lies.

Staying in a relationship
too long,
afraid of being together and afraid of being apart,
betraying myself, the real crime.

Lightning splits me open
to see truth lying fallow,
its subtle message—
use the light to let go.

Reading the Stars

Every time I wake up in the night
the stars are
in a different place
in the sky.

The first time I look out,
they are making the shape of a question mark.
What?? I ask out loud, smiling,
then fall back to sleep.

The second time I open my eyes,
I see a dusky smattering of stars,
tossed across the sky,
twinkling in their own mystery.

The third time I wake,
I just drink them in,
letting stars fill up
all the empty places in me.

The Balance

Swinging, powerfully
hand over hand through the jungle.
I must do everything myself.
Help must not be summoned.
Rest—not allowed.
Relentless pushing to the edge of exhaustion.

Illness teaches by taking away
swift, smooth moves.
The plug running energy
yanked from its socket.
My body appears
to betray me.

Longing to be finished,
shed this heavy girdle of bone and flesh,
yet a thin, retractable leash
jerks me back,
just when I want to speed free
of the plodding practice of being human.

Twilight, in childhood,
I stood high on a green metal fence,
queen of the backyard,
wrapped my hands around the T of the clothes pole,
pushed my body out as far as I could throw it,
then swung back to safety, the fence beneath my feet.

Delicate song of life,
when all seems too hard to bear . . .
Whisper me to stay—
remind me of the moments
when I reached up to touch
the tops of trees.

Song of Gila

I want to braid my hair with grass
so that the gray-green and gray-red
strands entwine.
Roll on my back,
let my limbs fall softly.
Become a part of the silence
that floats around me,
yet penetrates my being
like a radio wave from God.

Yellow dog scratches his collar,
wanting to be free.
Untie my own mask that stands
between me and love,
lay it carefully in the sun to shrivel and dry.
Lay, stomach-down,
nose to the ground,
breathing in the scent of grass,
where roots begin.

Attempted Relationship

You can't hate an apple
for being an orange.
You can be disappointed,
or even sad, if you want to.

You can tell yourself,
It felt so round . . .
But what about that bumpy skin
and that bright orange color?

All clues, ignored,
blinded by the crazy hope that
that this—
would be the perfect apple.

You could stand underneath
the apple tree and shout:
"Why can't you be what I imagined?"
After a while your throat gets sore.

You just keep writing,
compose new music,
love yourself,
and dance.

Revisit

When cutting the stalks of orange-tipped sorghum today,
the memory of the way I bent my body, held the knife,
pulled the stalks down and away,
came back to me.

The sway of the scythe, the hours
in the fields, sweat running down my back,
only sunset signaling the day's end,
walking home, laughing, tired, with the others.

Hiking through yellow river woods in fall
the smell of dry leaves, the swish
of dry grass, the soft sound of river nearby,
so familiar, tears come.

Something inside me, beyond logic,
beyond the mind,
knows I've lived before,
a spark, rekindled.

One

Watch the sun color the sky orange,
then yellow.
Heat bursts—
over the lip of the mountain to the east.

Tiny bird tracks are the ones you follow,
yellow and purple flowers cover the ground.
Make your body twist and bend
under a barb wire fence.

Weeding squash—next to tall, pink
zinnias, bells of blue-white sesame flowers.
Large black bees hum, while
butterflies dance above the rows.

The silence, so big
you can't find your place in it.
Then, one day—
it's part of you.

Head to the ditch in a roundabout way.
Even though the cool is what you want more than anything,
you wait, take your body in slowly,
feel the water ride up your thighs.

In the middle, where the water is deepest,
find a place where the creeks come together,
you—the land—the water—
touch.

Opening

The road rises up in front of you and all you can see is sky—
endless blue above you, opening itself to your vision,
You feel expanded, full of possibility, happy

to be part of this magnificent universe, smiling right along
with it.
When you reach the top of the hill, moving forward,
there is no time to plan or think,

you do not hesitate to press on the gas pedal
to move into a new realm, a new world of
discovering yourself, serving the Divine.

You trust, with a quick
intake of breath,
as you rise.

Lightning Splits the Sky

Another Door Calls to Me

In a semi-circle they stand,
brightly painted
yellow, green and orange,
all the doors, closed.
Plant myself in the dust
in front of them and watch
as the sun touches each of their faces,
illuminating my choices.

Toward nightfall, shadows begin to fall,
my mind becomes tired.
There is only one door that calls to me now,
the blue door.
It looks ancient, beaten,
with deep gouges in the wood
and scratches on the surface,
yet there is a faint glow around it.

When I put my hand around the old
metal knob, it's warm,
humming with electricity.
Remember to knock first,
asking permission to enter, and
only then does the knob turn.
Hinges creak, and I step into
a different world.

Three hallways greet me, as my foot
steps over the threshold.
They look the same,
so I start down the one on the left.

An eternal party blares in a haze of cigarette smoke,
people downing their drinks in gulps.
Too-loud music with the same beat plays over and over.
People lean in to whisper and gossip.
A woman with a half-filled glass in her hand beckons . . .
I turn, almost run, back to the entrance
and choose the hallway on the right.

An old couple sits on an couch in a bare living room,
listlessly watching T. V.
The woman gets up to go into the kitchen, the smell of
burning . . .
The man shouts gruffly, "When's dinner ready, woman?"
A feeling of cruelty, hopelessness and sorrow,
thick as the smell of grease, pervades the room.
I back out, retrace my steps
to find the entrance once more.

Only the hallway in the middle is left,
I sigh and follow.
Intense heat from the sun hits my back and

I'm standing in a dry creek bed of desert sand
with a high cliff on one side.
Around the bend, I see
random rows of stone indentations,
created by water over time,
long and curved, carved like shallow boats.

Rainwater covers the bottom of one of the stone oblongs,
and I ease myself down.
Nestled in the water,
gentled by the feel of water and sun,
each cell of my being moves toward peace.
Worries and dark thoughts dissolve into space.
Only my breathing in and breathing out—
call and response with the Source.

Can I stay?
Sharp call from raven breaks the silence.
Sudden knowing comes, I can return
just my closing my eyes—
anytime I wish.
Sit and look ahead, marveling at the endless possibilities,
then rise up and walk out,
looking back before my hand turns the knob to the door.
Close my eyes to arrange it all in my memory,
for the time I return.

Alive

This is who I am:
woman who drives with yellow dog
over roads of dirt,
going fast over dip of creek water.

Who is brown hills,
dry, sharp shrubs,
muddy river water,
smooth, worn stones on sand.

Strong as red rock cliff,
soft as grass,
uncertain as rain clouds,
brave as birdsong.

Turn right on the highway
back to town.
Don't lose this . . .
Don't lose this . . . .

THE PLACE BETWEEN LIGHT AND DARK

The trapeze swings out
and you have to let go.
In between can be a hard place,
meant to teach you to trust,
in something more than your own mind.

When your hands
slip from the bar—
do you see the one
whose wrists you can grasp,
flying toward you in the night?

The heart yearns to fly, to soar—
but you can't remember
how to be free.
Always hanging on so tight, afraid of the ride:
thrilling, risky, a little dangerous.

A gift lies buried beneath it all
Unwrap yourself from what you know,
let go and rise into the air,
into the deathless, exhilarating
moment of surrender where everything's all right.

Where love surrounds you, holds you,
and a woven net of blue light,
as big as your willingness to forgive,
waits—
with infinite patience.

Reality

Lightning splits the sky,
and thunder cracks an answer.
Rain pelts
the tent's thin skin:
my only protection.

Tired of trying to sleep,
I lie awake,
looking up,
when I feel rain
kiss my cheek.

A solitary drop
falls
through
my face,
and into the earth.

Supreme peace comes
and I breathe deeply,
smiling into the dark.

Who can I tell this to?
Who will understand the things
that happen beyond this plane
that are more real
than the brush of a hand?

Everything Begins in the Dark

Dark, protector of what needs shielding,
is just waiting
for the match to be struck,

the flame to burn bright,
the light to bring warmth,
the sun to come out.

A seed, gently placed inside the earth,
sun and rain slowly bring it to life,
until the seed's heart cracks open.

Energy that permeates all the worlds,
that speaks the language of pure love,
that opens the dry seed to life,

the same miracle
that splits open the seed's heart—
splits open mine.

Staying to the Middle

Even now, as she drives
down the steep highway,
she feels the edge call out to her.
She struggles to keep to the middle,
ignoring the voices,
the part that still calls her over.

Mountains with clouds
resting on their heads,
sky wider than the ocean,
brown land, dotted with pale sage,
the green smell of rain that falls to cleanse
each rock, leaf, and wandering soul.

Stretching eyes farther,
her spirit stretches to embrace all,
including herself, in a song of blessing.
As the sun rises,
she forgets to be afraid,
and lets the beauty carry her home.

Underground

When you walk
the dry, hot bed of a sandy arroyo,
imagine water running underground,
unseen, but nourishing,
feeding the ash trees, the little bushes,
the purple wildflowers.

When love doesn't appear
in the same form it once did,
it has not disappeared—
it has simply gone underground,
lost, not to your heart,
only to your vision.

One day it will spring up—
maybe not in the same place
or in the same way.
When your cat sits beside you,
puts her paw gently on your arm,
slowly a trickle begins to move, above ground.

Heartbeat of Sound

They gather up front, chairs in a half circle,
afternoon sun streaming in through the window,
light touching their hands as they find the beat on African drums,
plucking and strumming the strings of guitars and mandolin.

Men, finding chords and harmony,
sing of yearning, of death, of love.
No one is being harmed or threatened,
they all work together for the sake of a song.

The ones who listen become part of the music,
boots keeping time on the wooden floor,
hands tap on thighs, table-tops, voices join in on the chorus,
remembering words to the second verse.

A man yells at a little boy outside,
some of us get up to see if the boy's all right,
the music making a smooth passage
from strings, from sadness.

We are all working together,
with the afternoon sunlight streaming in,
light touching our faces as the music
becomes a new heartbeat, moving out into the world.

Dreaming Home

NEW VOICE

I have a new voice.
It is scratchy
and does not want to come out.
It is birthed in
fear of ridicule,
of torture
and shame.
It is raw
and I am afraid
of my own power.

Lost

Visiting the city, I feel locked inside its sprawl,
glass cutting me off from the outside world,
air conditioned cold chilling my body.
Outside, rows and rows of corn grow,
fertilized with chemicals,
beautiful, green, contaminated.

Concrete covers every road and walkway,
houses bump against each other,
apartments rise high to house thousands.
Freeways, thick with cars,
depend on gas pumps on every corner
to feed them all.

Random mechanical beeps,
fractured bits of sound,
resound inside stores,
and even vehicles,
pull me from my center.

Walking, I find a dirt road off the highway,
take my shoes off,
toes rejoice in squishy mud,
tall, yellow, flowering weeds grow
and I pick a few to remember
this small, wild space.

Inside at night, I breathe in small
shallow gasps.
Without the rhythm of the natural world,
without the exchange between
the earth, my senses, my heart,
I am lost.

Three deer

Three deer come out of my garden.
They may as well have the last of the tomatoes.
I silently ask them to leave
the pears and roses,
and they do.

The two young ones bound up the hill,
while the doe turns
to look at me in the dark.
We exchange a gaze of love
that seems to last longer
than hours or years.

When I return to bed,
I feel peaceful,
as if I'd caught
some of the deer's grace
and gentle purpose,

my whole being,
content,
in a new way
in this troubling time,
on this moonlit night.

SMALL BIRD

Near the garden
a small bird lands
on the top of a
tall, dry stalk.

She sits, head up,
as soft rain falls,
accepting everything.
I want to be like that.

My Dog Begins to Look Like a Wolf

He holds his head up,
then his nose rises
a little higher—
to sniff the air.
Satisfied no rain is coming,
he pauses, pees,
then walks slowly to the shade
to lie down.
Who is he, really?
An aged dog, almost fifteen,
with a tumor and
a fractured knee?
Or the dog with a
long line of wild ancestors?
He lies down now,
front paws stretched out,
his pointed teeth showing around the edge
of his tongue,
alert, watchful,
ears up, appearing
young and strong.
Underneath his yellow fur,
black fur of his ancestor,
the wolf, shows through.

I've seen him like this at the river,
finding his way downhill,
running fast and free over the sand,
biting his first mouthful of water,
then standing still,
watching, listening,
becoming part of the river,
becoming who he is.

All the little things

like watering the strawberries and currants,
because they are up and leafing,
or carrying the wicker basket,
full of wet clothes,
down the steps and out by the trees.
One could miss the way
the fingers squeeze together
the top of the clothespin to
attach the seam of the blue shirt
to the swaying clothesline.
One could miss the moment
when the sprinkler is moved around,
so that each small strawberry plant drinks in water,
up from its root tips.
One could miss these details of care,
one could look back over the day and say only
I washed the clothes,
I watered the garden.
One could miss all of these—
how the brown socks are
carefully laid out to dry.
I don't want to go on about it
but isn't it the small things,
the little acts of love,
that keep this
sacred world
spinning on its axis?

How it begins, how it ends

start loving right away in the morning,
realize this day is the only one you'll get.
contemplate, drink tea, read in the sun,
make a story, write it down,
wash the dishes,
sit on the swing,
follow the moon's path
through branches of the apricot tree.

keep loving far into the night,
even in your dreams.
feel the cat against your back.
imagine yourself living inside
a passionflower, a star, a sound.
now you exist everywhere—
quiet joy, your song.

Dreaming Home

Writing, moving above the earth
in a silver metal bird,
looking out the window, seeing pathways,
like lines scrawled on brown dirt
rise over hills.
Triangle mountaintop,
landmark in the distance,
dark outline against the glow of orange sunset.

Returning from the Midwest,
where green is the only color,
where water is abundant,
huge lakes everywhere.
The place I grew up,
have great love for,
have outgrown.

Below me,
thin thread of river meanders,
twisting through heat,
and red-brown dust.
The impossibility of flying
has come true,
broken through the wall of imagination into reality,
just as my dreams will.

About the Author

Elise Stuart moved to Silver City, New Mexico in 2005. She came to know the desert as a place where wild plants can survive without rain, a land where small yellow flowers grow in arroyos fed by underground streams. Reawakened to miracles of the natural world, she found her home.

In 2014, when she was chosen Poet Laureate of Silver City, she envisioned giving young people an opportunity to experience that same sense of connection and wonder. Inspired by the magic that the doors of poetry can open, beginning poets of all ages are now expressing themselves through the written and spoken word, participating in numerous activities and events, and creating a greater literary voice throughout the community.

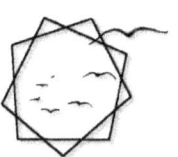

www.ingramcontent.com/pod-product-compliance
Lightning Source LLC
Chambersburg PA
CBHW022107040426
42451CB00007B/169